When They Think They Have Nothing to Write About . . .

(formerly published as *Cottonwood Composition Book*)

Cheryl Miller Thurston

Cottonwood Press, Inc.
Fort Collins, Colorado

Requests for permission should be addressed to:

Cottonwood Press, Inc.
305 West Magnolia, Suite 398
Fort Collins, CO 80521

ISBN 1-877673-00-5

Printed in the United States of America

Book design by Dawn DiPrince

Table of Contents

Using this Book

You know your students need to write more. But what should you have them write about?

It's hard to motivate the MTV generation. You hope to give assignments that inspire thought, creativity, wit, humor, excitement. Instead, you inspire questions like: "How long does it have to be?" and "Do we have to use ink?"

Now you have help: *When They Think They Have Nothing to Write About . . .* (formerly the *Cottonwood Composition Book)*. No, the book won't perform miracles. Your students aren't likely to become so excited about writing that they give up television, music, video games and the opposite sex. But they will be more likely to get involved in writing, to take an interest, to think and to *try.*

Best of all, the assignments in this book make things easier for you, the teacher.

Writing is a process.

The assignments in *When They Think They Have Nothing to Write About . . .* are based upon the widely-accepted theory that writing is, more or less, a three-step process:

1. Prewriting
2. Drafting
3. Revising and editing

Prewriting involves thinking, brainstorming, collecting information and deciding on a possible purpose or focus for the writing. Although this first step is often neglected, it is especially important for students. When they have trouble getting started, it is often because they have spent too little time preparing to write.

When They Think They Have Nothing to Write About . . . gives students special help with the prewriting process. Each complete assignment includes a "Getting Started" section that helps students come up with ideas and collect information to use in their first drafts.

The "Getting Started" activities often involve sharing with a partner or with members of small groups. Sharing increases motivation. The students get ideas from one another and have the added encouragement of an audience of peers. All in all, the "Getting Started" activities make the next step, drafting, much easier for most students.

Vary the assignments to suit your needs.

When They Think They Have Nothing to Write About . . . consists of two sections:

- Prewriting Plus — Complete Writing Activities for the Classroom
- 101 Quick Topics for Writing

"Prewriting Plus" activities help students write well-developed paragraphs or complete compositions. (You can assign paragraphs, short papers, or longer compositions, depending upon your purposes and the skills of your students.) They also require time — at least half a class period for the "Getting Started" exercise, plus additional time for writing, revising and editing. Most "Prewriting Plus" activities work best if the class spends at least one or two class periods on the total assignment, from start to finish.

Most of the assignments can be adapted for nearly any grade or ability level. However, the assignments with a star (★) beside the title tend to be more difficult, either because they take outside research, more preparation or more sophisticated thinking.

"101 Quick Topics for Writing" is full of quick writing topics that are perfect for journal or daybook entries, or for brief in-class writing assignments. They also can help students generate material to use later for longer compositions. You can photocopy pages and cut the short assignments apart for each student, or you can simply write the assignments on the board.

Keep it light.

Just as writing itself is a process, the teaching of writing is also a process. As teachers, we need to work *toward* goals, never expecting our students to master everything at once. It is better to encourage students to experiment, to think, to take risks — although they will make some mistakes along the way — than it is to have them write short, safe papers that are perfectly written but empty, devoid of thought, creativity or meaning.

So keep it light. Encourage your students to have some fun with the assignments in *When They Think They Have Nothing to Write About*. Type up interesting sentences or paragraphs from student papers and pass them out, trying to use material from as many papers as possible. Read aloud funny, interesting, exciting or moving papers. Post clever papers on the bulletin board. Try assignments yourself and share your results with the students. Talk. Laugh. Be silly. Be serious. Share ideas. Share results.

Your students will still ask, "How long does it have to be?" and "Do we have to use ink?" but they will also think, play with language, experiment and learn. In short, they will be on their way to becoming what we want them to be: thoughtful, effective writers.

Prewriting Plus —
Complete Writing Activities
for the Classroom

Name _____

The Trouble with Being a . . .

Suppose you weren't you at all. Suppose you were an inanimate object — a sock, a straw, a lawnmower, a toaster, a tube of lipstick, a fork, a locker, a bicycle, a lightbulb . . . anything.

Describe the problems you would encounter by being this object.

Getting Started

1. For three minutes, brainstorm. Write down every inanimate object you can think of. At the end of three minutes, meet with two other people and share your lists. Talk about which items might be the most interesting to write about. Then choose your subject.

2. Imagine how your view of the world would be different if you were the subject you have chosen. If you were a sock, for example, think about how most of you would usually be enclosed in a shoe, fitted around a foot, perhaps a smelly foot. How would you feel about being in that position? What things would make you mad? What problems can you imagine?

3. Think of the five senses. What would you *see, hear, taste, smell* and *feel* if you were the inanimate object you have chosen?

Name _____

Scared to Death

Think of a time when you were afraid. Did you have a nightmare? Was someone you know in an accident? Did you think someone was breaking into your house? Were you watching a horror movie? Were you afraid of getting up in front of a group? Were you worried about what your parents were going to do about something you had done wrong?

Describe a time you were afraid, using details to create a "picture" of the situation that caused your fear.

Getting Started

1. Think back to the way you felt when you were afraid. Physically, what happened to you? Was your throat dry? Were you sick to your stomach? Did your palms get sweaty? Did your heart beat faster? Were you frozen, unable to move?

2. What thoughts went through your mind when you were afraid? What did you do? What did you say? What did others do and say?

3. Choose a partner and tell that person what happened to make you afraid. Have your partner ask you questions to help you think of more details.

Name _____

An Absolutely Perfect Day

Imagine that you could wake up tomorrow and have an absolutely perfect day. What would happen? Who would you see? Where would you go? What would you do?

Describe your absolutely perfect day.

Getting Started

1. Think of the good days you have had in the past. What happened to make those days special?

2. Brainstorm for five minutes. Writing as fast as you can, list every good thing you can possibly think of to include in your day. Here are some things to consider:

   - What would you eat?

   - What would you wear?

   - How would people treat you? What kinds of things would they say to you?

   - How would you act?

   - What would you say?

   - Where would you go? How would you get there?

Include anything you can think of that would make your day perfect.

Name _____

Sick! Sick! Sick!

If you're like most people, you hate being sick, unless you're just a *little* bit sick. Being a little bit sick means you're just sick enough to stay home from school, but not too sick to enjoy the day off!

Think about the times you have been sick or injured. Do you remember having the chicken pox? The mumps? The flu? A cough that wouldn't go away? The worst sore throat in the world? A broken bone? Stitches?

Write about your most miserable (or memorable) illness or injury.

Getting Started

1. Think about the following questions:

    *   How did you feel? What was your worst symptom?

    *   If you had an accident, what happened?

    *   Who took care of you?

    *   When did you first start feeling ill? Where were you?

    *   Was there anything unusual about your illness? For example, did your whole family get sick at the same time? Did you break a bone you had never heard of before? Did you require unusual treatment?

2. Tell a partner about your illness. Encourage your partner to ask questions that will help you remember details.

3. Interview someone else about your illness to find out what that person remembers. You might talk to your mother or father, a brother or sister, a neighbor, a teacher, anyone who was there and might remember something you don't recall.

Name _____

School Days, School Days

Going to school for the first time is a big event in every child's life. Because of that, most of us have vivid memories of our first days in school. Think back to your very first days in kindergarten or first grade. What do you remember? What stands out in your mind?

Write about one of your earliest memories of school.

Getting Started

1. Try free writing. For five minutes, write as fast as you can, recording everything you can remember about your first memory or memories of school. Don't worry about spelling or punctuation or handwriting. Let your mind go wherever it wants, and try to get as much as you can down on paper in the time allowed.

2. Talk to your parents or other relatives about what *they* remember about your first days of school. How did you act? What incidents or details do they remember?

3. Think about the following questions:

   - What did you wear on the first day of school?

   - Did you get to buy anything special for school, like a new notebook or lunch box?

   - How did your parents act? How about your brothers or sisters?

   - What was your teacher like?

   - What boys and girls do you remember?

   - Did anything embarrassing happen? Anything funny? Anything exciting?

   - Did anything puzzle or confuse you?

   - What do you remember doing in school during class time? How about during recess?

   - What was the *best* thing about going to school?

Name _____

The Worst!

During the many years we spend in school, all of us have teachers that we like less than others. That's only natural. Think about all the teachers you have had in the past. Who do you think is the worst teacher you have had so far?

Describe your worst teacher as clearly as you can, using details to make the person "come alive" on paper. (Do not use the teacher's real name. Call the person Mr. or Ms. X, or make up an outrageous name of your own.)

Getting Started

1. Tell a partner about your worst teacher. Then listen to your partner tell about his or her worst teacher. Ask each other questions to get more information.

2. Think about the following questions:

   - What did you dislike about this teacher?

   - Can you remember some specific things the teacher did that upset you?

   - Did the teacher have any annoying habits? If so, what?

   - Did you feel you were singled out or treated differently by this teacher? If so, in what way?

   - How did you feel when you came into this teacher's class? Bored? Angry? Embarrassed? Hurt? Frustrated? Disappointed? Amused? Other reactions?

   - Was there anything about the teacher's appearance or voice that bothered you?

   - How did others feel about the teacher?

   - Did you learn from the teacher? If so, why? If not, why not?

   - What was the teacher's *best* quality?

Name _____

What to Do with a Glopsnerch

You have just given someone a glopsnerch. This person is not at all familiar with glopsnerches. Only you are.

Write instructions to go with your gift. Describe what to do with a glopsnerch, explaining very carefully everything that is important to know.

Remember: Only *you* know what a glopsnerch is!

Getting Started

1. Think about the following questions:

   - Is a glopsnerch large or small?

   - Is it an animal, a plant, a machine, an object or what?

   - To whom are you giving this glopsnerch — a friend, a relative, an enemy, an acquaintance? Why are you giving it to this person?

   - What special characteristics does your glopsnerch have? Does it have special talents or capabilities or needs? Does it require special care?

   - What is the *best* thing to do with a glopsnerch?

2. Draw a picture of your glopsnerch. Include diagrams or illustrations for its use, if necessary. You may want to turn in your picture with your final paper.

Name _____

Three Wishes

Many people daydream about finding a magic lantern or meeting a fairy god-mother who will give them anything they want. Suppose it really happened. Suppose you were given the chance to have three wishes granted — any three wishes in the world. What would you wish for?

Describe your three wishes and explain why you would choose each.

Getting Started

1. For five minutes, brainstorm. Write down everything you can think of that you would like to have — things, qualities, personality traits, *anything*. Don't worry about spelling or punctuation or handwriting. Just try to write for the whole five minutes.

2. Think about the following questions:
   - What places would you like to visit?
   - What would you like to see happen in your life?
   - What things would you like to buy, if you had the money?
   - What changes would you like to see occur, either in yourself, in other people or in the world?
   - What else can you think of that you would like to have?

3. Get together with three other students and tell about your wishes. Describe each wish. For example, if you wished for a car, what make would it be? What color? Where would you drive it? If you wished for a happy life, tell what happiness means to *you*.

Name _____

★ The Week I Was Born ★

Find a magazine published the week you were born — or better yet, a newspaper from the *day* you were born. Look through it, noting important events, unusual stories, advertisements, the comics, etc.

Write about any *one* observation you can make about the week (or day) you were born.

or

Tell about the major news events of the week (or day) you were born.

Getting Started

1. As you read your newspaper or magazine, see if you note any similarities or differences in the stories, or between what was happening then and what is happening now. Here are some examples of observations you might make:

   - The week I was born was a violent one. (What happened?)

   - Sports were really making headlines the week I was born. (Explain.)

   - A woman dominated the news the week I was born. (Who? Why?)

   - During the week I was born, the most unusual story in the news concerned two alligators (Why? What happened?)

   - The news the week I was born was very similar to the news of this week. (How? What was happening then? Now?)

   - Comic strips have really changed since I was born. (How? What is different?)

   - Advertisements look very different today than they did the week I was born. (How? What is different?)

2. Show your newspaper or magazine to another adult and ask questions about the events described. Does the adult remember any more about the items — or about what happened afterwards? (If you can't check out the newspaper or magazine from the library, make a copy or jot down some questions to ask an adult about later.)

Name _____

Monsters! #1

Create a monster — the most terrible, frightening monster you can imagine. Perhaps, in some ways, your monster will resemble monsters you have seen on television or in movies. But be sure to make your monster a new one, one that *you* have invented.

Describe what your monster looks like, using words that will show just how awful it really is.

Getting Started

1. Talk with a partner about monsters you have read about or seen on television or in movies. What kinds of monsters were the most frightening to you?

2. Think about the following questions:

   - How tall is your monster? What shape? What color?

   - Is your monster primarily an animal, a human, a machine, a ghost, an extra-terrestrial or something else?

   - What is most frightening about the monster?

   - What unusual features does it have?

   - If you were to touch the monster, what would it feel like? What kinds of sounds would it make?

   - Where does the monster live?

   - What is the monster called?

3. Draw a picture of your monster. You may want to turn in your picture with your finished paper.

Name _____

Monsters! #2

In Monsters! #1, you created a monster. Now imagine that monster in motion. How would it act? What would it do? What would happen to things or people around it?

Describe your monster in action or in motion. You might tell how it walks, sleeps, eats, destroys or does whatever it is that it does best.

Getting Started

1. Think about the following questions:

   - Imagine how your monster moves. Is it quick? Slow? Graceful? Awkward?

   - What happens to things that get in its path?

   - What sounds do you hear as your monster moves?

   - What colors do you see?

   - How do people or animals or objects react to it?

   - Does it have any unusual powers?

   - Does it carry anything? If so, what?

   - What does your monster do best?

2. Using each of the five senses, describe what happens when your monster acts. What do you hear? What do you smell? Do you taste anything? What do you feel? What do you see?

3. Draw a picture of your monster in motion. You may want to turn in your picture with your final paper.

Name _____

The Big Shrink

All of us have felt angry towards someone. Many of us have also felt angry because we were afraid to speak up, or because we couldn't think of anything to say until later.

Imagine that a person who has made you angry has shrunk to only one-inch tall. You hold this tiny person in the palm of your hand, and he or she is at your mercy. Think about what you will tell the person.

Now, write what you will say. (It may be a good idea to use a pseudonymn instead of the person's name.)

Getting Started

1. Think about the following questions:

    *   Who are some people who have made you angry? What happened to make you angry?

    *   Do you want to "get back" at someone, or do you just want this person to understand your feelings? Why?

    *   Do you want to get someone to make some promises or changes? If so, what promises? What changes?

    *   Do you want the person to learn a lesson? If so, what lesson?

    *   Do you want to be a different kind of person than you usually are with this person? If so, what kind of person would you like to be?

Name _____

★ Baby Face ★

When most people write autobiographies, they write about things they can remember about their lives. But think about all those years you can't remember — from the time you were born until you were three or four. A lot happened then, whether you remember it or not.

Do some research and find out about those years you don't remember. Talk to people who *do* remember. Ask questions. Then write an autobiography of yourself when you were very, very small from birth until age three or four.

Getting Started

1. Ask questions. Talk to people, anyone who knew you as a baby. Try your parents, grandparents, neighbors, brothers and sisters. Here are a few questions you might ask:

    *   How did your parents announce your birth?

    *   Were you a cranky baby? An "easy" baby?

    *   What were your favorite foods? Toys? Did you have a favorite blanket or other item that you had to have with you all the time?

    *   Did you have any imaginary friends?

    *   When did you first talk? What was your first word? Who heard it?

    *   What trouble did you get into as a small child?

    *   Did you ever embarrass your family? How?

    *   How did any brothers and sisters feel about your birth? Were they jealous? Proud of you? Did they spoil you? Resent you?

    *   Did you have a favorite baby-sitter?

    *   Did you ever throw a temper tantrum? About what?

    *   Did you go through the "terrible twos"? How did you act?

    *   What is your earliest memory? How old do you think you were?

2. Dig out old photo albums and your baby book, if you have them. What can you learn from the items included?

3. If you were adopted, write about the first knowledge you have about your childhood or about the adoption itself.

Name _____

Bare Bones #1

Your writing is much more effective when you use specific, interesting words — in other words, details.

For example, here is a sentence that tells us something, but not much:

The child misbehaved.

Here is a sentence that gives us the same information, but in a much more interesting, informative way:

When his mother told him he couldn't have the Hershey bar, the spoiled toddler plopped down in the middle of the supermarket and shrieked so loudly that three sackers, two checkers and the assistant manager rushed over to see what had happened.

Below is a bare-bones story — a story with only basic information. Rewrite the story, keeping the same essential facts, but adding details to make it interesting.

A boy sat down at the table in the building. He ate the food. A girl watched him. She had strong feelings about what she saw. She spoke to the boy.

Getting Started

1. Think about the kind of story you want to create. Was the boy a teenager or a child? What was he eating? How was he eating it? How old was the girl? What did she think of the boy? When she spoke, was she rude, friendly, teasing or what?

2. After you have your first draft, go back and see if you can change some words to more interesting ones. For example, could you change the word "boy" to "brat" or "football player"? Could you change "building" to "McDonald's Restaurant" or "doghouse" or "the Empire State Building"?

Name _____

Bare Bones #2

Your writing is much more effective when you use specific, interesting words — in other words, details.

For example, here is a sentence that tells us something, but not much:

The boy asked the girl a question.

Here is a sentence that gives us the same information, but in a much more interesting, informative way:

With sweat pouring down his scarlet face, Scott walked up to Jennifer and blurted, "Would you like to go to a movie tonight? I mean, with me? I mean, you know, like on a date? Or something?"

Below is a bare-bones story — a story with only basic information. Rewrite the story, keeping the same essential facts, but adding details to make it interesting.

Two vehicles approached an intersection. Neither stopped. They collided. There was a lot of noise. There was destruction. The drivers of the vehicles got out and approached one another. They were very angry. They argued. The police came.

Getting Started

1. Think about the kind of story you want to create. What kind of vehicles were they — cars, trains, trucks? Why didn't they stop? What did the noise sound like? What kind of damage was there? How did the drivers look as they approached one another? Where they male or female? How old were they? What did they say when they argued? How did the police handle them?

2. After you have your first draft, go back and see if you can change some words to more interesting ones. For example, could you change "car" to "Ferrari" or "Volkswagen Bug" or "Model T"? Could you change "driver" to a "a teenage girl with braces on her teeth" or "a middle-aged man in a jogging suit"?

Bare Bones #3

Your writing is much more effective when you use specific, interesting words — in other words, details.

For example, here is a sentence that tells us something, but not much:

The teacher looked at the student.

Here is a sentence that give us the same information, but in a much more interesting, informative way:

Mrs. Hogarty fixed her icy stare on Leslie, who, instead of multiplying decimals, was innocently drawing pictures of her teacher dressed as a witch.

Below is a bare-bones story — a story with only basic information. Rewrite the story, keeping the same essential facts, but adding details to make it interesting.

The baby-sitter was alone in the living room. There was a noise at the window. She lifted the curtain and looked outside. She saw something. She screamed.

Getting Started

1. Think about the kind of story you want to create. How old was the baby-sitter? What kind of home was she in? What kind of noise did she hear? What did she see when she lifted the curtain?

2. After you have your first draft, go back and see if you can change some words to more interesting ones. For example, could you change "house" to "Victorian mansion" or "rambling farmhouse"? Could you change "curtain" to "silken drapes" or "tattered dish towel hanging over the window"?

Name _____

A Martian's First Impressions of Earth

You are a Martian who has just landed on earth for the first time. What do you see? What do you hear? What do you make of it all?

In a letter to a fellow Martian back home, describe your first impressions of earth.

Getting Started

1. First, think about yourself as a Martian. What do you look like? How are you similar to earthlings? How are you different?

2. Now, think about the earth. Answer the following questions:

   • Where exactly have you landed? Is it on a mountain? In a river? In a city? On a highway? On a rooftop? In an amusement park? Wherever it is, be specific. If it's on a farm, *where* on the farm is it — the top of the barn, a cornfield, the pig's feeding trough?

   • Imagine what you see as you look around you. Are you sure who the earthlings are? What do you think of them?

   • How do you feel? Are you afraid? Amused? Impressed? Disappointed? Why?

   • What surprises you about earth?

   • What else can you tell your friend on Mars about the planet earth?

3. Draw a picture or diagram to go with your letter, showing earth from a Martian point-of-view.

Oldest/Youngest/Only

Are you the oldest of your brothers and sisters? The youngest? In the middle? An only child?

Older brothers and sisters often think their parents are easier on the youngest child. The youngest child often complains that nothing he or she does is ever special because an older brother or sister has already done it. Middle children often think that they don't get as much attention as other children.

People from big families sometimes imagine how wonderful it would be to get all the attention of an only child. And, of course, people with no brothers and sisters often imagine how nice it would be to have dozens of them.

What do you think? Is it best to be the oldest, the youngest, in the middle or an only child?

Explain what position you think is best. Imagine that you are trying to convince someone who disagrees with you.

Getting Started

1. Find someone who disagrees with you, and listen to that person's reasons for disagreeing.

2. Think about the following questions:

   - What is your position in your family? How do you feel about being in that position?

   - Do you think someone else in your family has it easier than you do? If so, in what way? Does it have anything to do with being older or younger than you?

   - What are the advantages of being in your position? The disadvantages?

   - If you could switch positions for a day, what would be the best thing about your new position? The worst thing?

Name _____

★ The Time Capsule ★

The President of the United States has created a Blue Ribbon Time Capsule Committee. The commitee includes 25 members representing a cross-section of American culture. Each of the committee members has a task: to choose three items to include in a time capsule that will be opened 500 years from now. The President wants the committee members to choose items that will help future human beings understand what life is like in America today.

You have been chosen as one of the committee members for the Blue Ribbon Time Capsule Committee. What three items will you choose to include in the time capsule — and why?

Describe your three selections and defend your choices in a letter to the President.

Getting Started

1. Imagine the people 500 years from now who might open the time capsule. They are likely to be very different from us, living in a very different sort of world. In a small group, discuss the following questions:

   - What language changes might have taken place 500 years from now?

   - How might the environment be different?

   - Will the people necessarily be more technologically advanced than we are? Why or why not?

   - Do you think the people might be physically different from us? If so, in what ways?

   - How might differences between these people and present-day people create problems in understanding? In what ways?

2. For each category below, list items that might tell future generations something about America today. (For example, under "People" you might list a picture of the President or some other influential person.)

Movies	Magazines	Machines	Plants	Animals	Books
People	Objects	Sports	Games	Clothing	Other

3. In a small group, share what items you have listed in the categories above. Discuss which items might be best to include in the time capsule. Then, individually, narrow your choices to three items.

Name _____

★The Rock Concert★

Imagine that a family sits down to watch television, and they watch five minutes of a rock concert given by a popular group. After five minutes, the mother or father insists on changing the channel, although the son or daughter doesn't want to change. There is an argument.

Now try imagining this scene from different points of view. First, imagine that you are the mother or father. Write about the scene from his or her point of view.

Now imagine that you are the son or daughter. Write about the scene from his or her point of view.

Now imagine that you are a third party — a visitor, the dog, even an inanimate object like the sofa. Write about the scene from that party's point of view.

Getting Started

1. Imagine the scene. How many are in this family? Where are they sitting? What rock group are they watching? What kind of person is the mother? The father? How old is the son or daughter? What kind of argument is it — short, loud, good-natured, furious or what?

2. Make a list of things about the concert that family members might view differently. Some examples might be hairstyles, language, music lyrics or the audience.

3. Before you write from the point of view of a character, sit back, close your eyes, and try to think as that character might think. Then begin to write, saying the things that you think the character would be likely to say.

Name _____

Artifacts

Pretend you are a scientist from the future — 500 years in the future. You have just dug up one of today's touch-tone telephones, though, of course, you don't know that's what it is. Now you must write a report on the telephone for a scientific journal.

Describe what you believe the telephone to be. Discuss what kind of people you think used it and how — and for what purpose — they used it. There is one catch, though: You can't say it was used as a telephone.

Getting Started

1. Take three minutes and brainstorm every use you can think of for a telephone. Put *anything* you can think of down, no matter how silly. At the end of three minutes, share your list with a partner.

2. Name your artifact.

3. Look at all the parts of the telephone and imagine what uses a future scientist might see for them. What might the cord be used for? The buttons? The receiver?

4. Choose what you, the future scientist, believe the telephone to be. List all the reasons you can think of to support your belief.

Name _____

★ You — In Twenty Years ★

Imagine yourself twenty years from now. What do you think you will be like? What do you think your life will be like?

Try to be realistic in your predictions. Don't say that you will probably be living on Mars if you know that's just a crazy dream. If, on the other hand, that's something you really believe likely, go ahead and write about it.

Don't be afraid to set high goals, but also consider them in light of what you know about yourself — your strengths, your limitations, your resources, and the world around you.

Now write about yourself, describing your future life as you imagine it.

Getting Started

1. Interview at least three adults over age 30. Write down and think about their answers to the following questions:

   - What surprises you most about your life today?

   - What advice would you give to people your age about preparing for the future — other than to do your best in school?

   - How is being an adult different from what you thought it would be like when you were younger?

   - What is one of the most important things you have learned in the last ten years?

2. Now think about yourself. Answer the following questions:

   - What do you imagine you will be doing for a living?

   - Where will you live?

   - What will be important to you?

   - What problems and worries do you think you will have?

   - How will you be like your parents?

   - How will you be different from your parents?

   - What's one thing you know, absolutely, that will be true about you?

★ Interviewing ★

People are one of the most interesting sources of information around. The best way to learn from people is, of course, to ask them questions.

Set up an appointment to interview someone who interests you or someone who knows a lot about a subject that interests you. Be sure to write out the interview questions ahead of time.

Write about your interview. What did you learn? What did you find most interesting? What surprised you?

Getting Started

1. First you need to find someone to interview. Get together with a partner to talk about possible subjects. There are lots of possibilities. Here are just a few:

   - Interview a person in a career you are interested in. Find out about the benefits and drawbacks of the job.

   - Interview an older relative about what your mother or father was like as a child.

   - Interview a student who has a skill you admire — playing the drums, shooting baskets, dancing, etc. Find out how he or she developed that skill.

   - Interview a person over age 60 about what life was like when he or she was young.

   - Interview a person from another country — or someone who has visited another country — to find out how life is different there from in the U.S.

   - Interview someone you admire, to find out more about that person's life, and perhaps to get ideas about how to conduct your own life, as well.

2. Design your questions. It is important to choose questions that require more than a "yes" or "no" answer. Before you go to the interview, go over your questions with a partner and see if you can improve any of them.

3. Go through the material you have collected from the interview. Decide what you want to include in your paper and what you want to leave out. Do you see any over-all pattern, any major theme or idea that keeps coming up? Perhaps you could base your paper on that.

When you are finished with your paper, write the person you interview a short thank-you note for the interview. Send along a paragraph or two from your paper, or — if you don't mind sharing the whole thing — send a copy of the entire paper.

Name _____

★ An Autobiography — of Just *Part* of You ★

Nearly everyone has written an autobiography of some type. Usually these autobiographies include the same information: where you were born, who your parents are, where you went to school, how many brothers and sisters you have, etc.

Sometimes it's fun to try a different kind of autobiography — an autobiography of just *part* of you. Concentrating on just one area, you can go into greater depth and perhaps even learn some things about yourself. Try one of these topics for an autobiography of just part of you:

- A Language Autobiography
- A Sports Autobiography

Getting Started

1. If you are writing a language autobiography, think about your life in relation to words — speaking them, reading them and writing them.

   - What do you remember about learning language and language skills? When did you say your first word? What was it? What do your parents or others who knew you remember?

   - What do you remember about learning to read and write?

   - Did you have favorite books, poems, songs or phrases when you were younger?

   - Have you ever had an experience with a foreign language? How did that affect you?

   - How did school affect your feelings about reading and writing? Do you remember your first trip to the library?

   - Have words ever gotten you into trouble or embarrassed you?

2. If you are writing a sports autobiography, think about your life in relation to sports.

   - Are sports important to you? How? Why? How important has competition been to you?

   - How did you first become involved in sports or athletic activities? What are you earliest memories? Were you good at something right away?

   - Have you ever been bad at sports, at sports in general or at a particular sport? What is your best sport now? In the past?

   - How have you changed or improved over the years? How have sports affected your overall growth?

   - Has participation in sports ever worried, frightened or bothered you in any way?

Name _____

★ An Opinion Poll ★

Conduct a survey of your classmates on a topic that interests you. Make it more than just an opinion poll, though. Find out *reasons* for the opinions.

After you collect your results, see if you see any patterns. Is there anything that surprises you? Do you see different answers from boys and girls, or from students in different grade levels?

Write a paper describing and discussing the results of your survey.

Getting Started

1. First you need to think of a subject for your survey. Pick something that you find interesting. Would you like to know what your classmates think about a controversial issue? Would you like to know what they see as a solution to a school or community problem? Would you like to know what they think makes a person popular? What about favorite daydreams, favorite rock groups, favorite songs? Meet with a partner and brainstorm some subjects for a survey.

   Note: If you are going to question a large number of people, you may want to work with three or four other students on the same poll. However, each of you should write separate papers describing and discussing your results.

2. After you pick a subject, have your teacher approve it. Then design your survey and plan how you will conduct it. Think about the following questions:

   • Will you need to get permission from anyone before conducting the survey?

   • Are you going to pass out a questionnaire to the whole class, to several classes, to people at lunch? If so, how are you going to get copies? Who will pass out the questionnaires? Who will collect them? How will you tally the results?

   • Perhaps you will want to interview just a few people, asking them more in-depth questions. If so, how are you going to choose those people? What questions are you going to ask them?

101

Quick Topics
for
Writing

Pride

Describe a time you felt proud of yourself. Don't be modest. What did you do? Was it difficult? Did you get any recognition? How did others react to you?

Bigger

When is bigger *not* better?

School Year

Agree or disagree: The school year should be lengthened so that it is as long as those in Japan and many European countries.

Not Nearly

I'm not nearly as _____ as I'd like to be when . . .

Good Old Days

To me, one thing that sounds good about the "good old days" is . . .

A Mistake

Write about a mistake you have made. Was it a mistake in judgment, a mistake on a test or in a contest, a mistake that had lasting consequences or some other kind of mistake? What happened? How did you feel? What did you learn?

Advice

I have some sound advice. Never . . .

Testimonial

Choose a specific product that you use and like. Pretend you have just been hired by the manufacturer to write a new magazine ad or a television commercial for that product. Try to convince the public that your product is best, the one they should buy. Your product might be a certain model of car, an athletic shoe, the hamburgers sold at a fast food chain, a type of jeans or something else that interests you.

Remember, *you* have been hired to do the advertising, so you don't want your ad or commercial to resemble those that may already exist for this product.

Forgiving

One thing I have a very hard time forgiving is . . .

Vacation Time

Most people are sick of writing about "What I Did on My Vacation." Perhaps you are one of those people whose vacation just wasn't all that exciting.

So try the same topic with a twist: "What I WISH I had Done on My Vacation." With this one anything is possible!

Six Years Old

The best part about being six years old again would be . . .

A Magic Machine

Think of a chore or job you hate — whether it's a school job like math homework or a home job like drying the dishes. Invent a machine to do that chore. Now write the copy for a magazine ad selling your wonderful new machine.

Remember to consider your audience. For example, if you think the best potential market for your product would be young mothers, you will probably write a very different ad than if you want to reach 14-year-old boys. It's important to write an ad that will appeal to the people you want to buy your product.

Experience

If there's one thing I have learned, it's that . . .

Let Me!

What do you want to do that you're not allowed to do? Convince a person in authority that you should be allowed to do it.

For example, you might try to convince your parents that you should be allowed to stay out later or to go on dates. You might try to convince a teacher that you should be allowed to eat in class or retake a test. You might try to convince the principal to allow you to leave school grounds at lunch, to drop English or to wear shorts to school.

Try to come up with the best arguments you can for *your* position.

Friends

My friend's most outstanding quality is his or her . . .

If I Were Principal . . .

Imagine that you have suddenly become principal of your school. Describe the changes you will make in the school.

Are there school policies you will change? Will you treat students differently? Will you treat teachers differently? Will you make different rules? Will you change the physical make-up of the school? What things will you keep the same? Why? What results do you think your changes will bring?

Television

What makes _____ such a good television show is . . .

Color Me

Choose a color. You know what it looks like. But suppose you had to describe the color to someone who can't see. How would you do it?

You probably couldn't, not accurately. But what you might do is give the person a "feel" for the color by using senses other than sight to describe it.

For example, what might your color feel like if you could touch it? What might it smell like, taste like, sound like? If it had a personality, what type or personality might it have? What might it think or dream about? What might it do for fun?

Parenting

When I am a parent, one thing I'll never do is . . .

Winter Holiday

How does your family spend the winter holidays? Do you celebrate Christmas? Hanukkah? The new year? What traditions do you follow? What are your favorite traditions? Do you have a traditional dinner, party, religious ceremony?

Describe a typical winter holiday for your family.

Influence

A person who has had a big influence on me, other than my mother or my father, is . . .

Battle of the Sexes

(For girls) Boys have it easy. They don't have to . . .

or

(For boys) Girls have it easy. They don't have to . . .

Father

I hope I turn out like my father when it comes to his . . .

A Special Gift

Describe a gift that meant a lot to you. Why was the gift special? Was it the gift itself, the circumstances or the giver that meant the most to you?

Had you been expecting the gift? Had you done something to deserve it? Why was this gift different from others?

Mother

I hope I turn out like my mother when it comes to her . . .

Car of Your Dream

It's ten years from today, and you have just won the lottery. You are going to buy the car of your dreams. Describe it.

Remember — technology is ten years more advanced that it is today. You may be able to have a car with many features that aren't available today.

Worries

I worry about . . .

What's "In"

Look around you at popular haircuts, clothing styles or other fads involving appearance. Which ones do you like most? Which ones do you dislike? Why? Which ones do you think will look ridiculous 25 years from now?

Just Me

Sometimes I feel like I'm the only person around who . . .

Music Video

Think about music videos. Do you like to watch them? Why or why not? How do they affect your feelings about a song? Have you ever been surprised by a video of a song you have heard before? What surprised you? Have you ever liked a song more because of the video? Less? Explain.

Boredom

The most boring thing in the world to me is . . .

Expectations

What expectations do others have for you? Are they too high? Too low? How do you feel about those expectations?

Fear

What scares me is . . .

The Plus Side

The best thing about school is . . .

When I Was Young . . .

Children often get ideas that seem strange, at least to adults. For example, some children think tiny people live in the television set or that wind is caused by the trees flapping their branches. What unusual ideas did you have as a child?

Changes

One thing I wish I could change about myself is . . .

Star Appeal

How is a hero different from a star or a well-known personality? Are they ever the same thing?

If Only . . .

If only there weren't . . .

Fame

If I could be famous person for a day, I think I'd like to be . . .

Summarizing

Read about something interesting that has happened in the news recently. Find out about the event from three different sources, one of which may be television or radio.

Now, in your own words, describe what happened, pretending you are writing for someone your own age who hasn't heard anything about this event. (Note: It's a good idea to include the five W's — Who, What, When, Where and Why.)

Brothers and Sisters

The best thing about brothers or sisters is . . .

A Secret Kindness

If you had the power to do something really nice for someone, anonymously, what would you do? Why?

Sibling Rivalry

The worst things about brothers and/or sisters is . . .

One of a Kind

There's no one like . . .

Embarrassment

Nobody can write about his or her most embarrassing moment. It's too embarrassing! Instead, write about an embarrassing moment that you are willing to share. What happened? Who witnessed it? Why was it so embarrassing?

Mysteries

I can't understand why . . .

Rip Van Winkle

Like Rip Van Winkle, you have slept for 100 years. You now wake up. What do you see? How is the world different? What surprises you? How do people react to you?

School

This school would be a better place if . . .

Anger

I really get angry when . . .

Dreams

Describe a dream you remember having. What happened? Who was in the dream? What was the best part of the dream? The worst? Why do you think you had such a dream? Did it have some meaning or message for you?

The Minus Side

The worst thing about school is . . .

What I *Don't* Want to Be When I Grow Up

You may not be sure yet of what you want to be as an adult. But most students have a good idea what they *don't* want to be. What are you sure you don't want to be? Why?

Santa Claus

How did you find out there is no Santa Claus? What happened? Who told you? How did you feel? How did you act?

Sadness

I feel sad when . . .

Home

Describe a place where you feel psychologically at home. For example, is it in the big bean bag chair in your basement, in an old treehouse, at a certain spot on the beach or in your own room at home? Why is your special place so comfortable to you? What do you like to do there?

Picky, Picky

This may seem picky, but I really hate . . .

Conflict

Describe a conflict you have recently witnessed — like a fight, an argument or a close football game, for example. What was the conflict about? What happened? What was said? Who appeared to win?

Confusion

I feel really confused when I . . .

Travel Trip

Where in the world would you like to travel? Why? Do you think you ever will?

No More Adults!

Suppose there were a law saying that teenagers no longer had to pay any attention to parents, teachers or other adults. What do you think would happen? Why? How would you feel about such a law? What would be its strengths? Its weaknesses?

Promises

Agree or disagree: Sometimes a person should break a promise.

Animals

If you were to turn into an animal tomorrow, what animal would you be? Why?

Weird Elmer

Pretend that you have an incredibly weird friend named Elmer, and no one knows about him. Describe what Elmer is like. What makes him weird? Why is he your friend?

Caught!

Describe a time you got caught. For example, were you ever caught cheating, lying, disobeying, playing a trick, doing something embarrassing? What happened as a result? How did you feel?

Reading Minds

Suppose you — and only you — had the power to read people's minds. What problems can you imagine? What advantages would you have over others? Do you think you would like having such a power? Why or why not?

G-Rated?

Agree or disagree: Music tapes and CDs should have ratings, like movies.

Movie Ratings

Agree or disagree: Movie ratings like "R," "PG," etc. are a good idea.

Life or Death

Agree or disagree: People should be kept alive by machines even when there is no hope for recovery.

Vacation Blues

Describe the low point in a vacation or trip you have taken, even if it was just a trip to the mall. What happened? Why was it the low point? How did you feel?

Little Mysteries

Life has many mysteries, like "Where do missing socks from the washer and dryer go?" or "Why does it always rain right after you wash the car?" What little mysteries puzzle you?

Honesty

Agree or disagree: No one is really honest.

Dating

Agree or disagree: Some parents won't allow their children to date until they are age 16. Most parents should adopt this rule for their own children.

Drinking

Agree or disagree: The drinking age in our state should be raised.

English

Agree or disagree: English should not be a required class in our school.

Live Action

What sport do you most like to play? Why? Are you any good? What do you enjoy about it? What sport do you least like to play? Why?

Smoking

Agree or disagree: Cigarette smoking should be banned altogether in our community.

Voting

Agree or disagree: The voting age should be lowered to 13 because teenagers are as capable of voting as anyone else.

Horoscopes

Agree or disagree: Reading horoscopes is a ridiculous waste of time.

Driving

Agree or disagree: If they can pass the driving test, teenagers should be allowed to get a driver's license at age 13.

Watching Sports

What is the best sport to watch? Why? Is your answer different depending on if you're watching in person or watching on television?

Curfews

Agree or disagree and tell why: Curfews are ridiculous. Young people over the age of 12 should be able to decide for themselves what time to come home.

Compare

Compare yourself to a certain animal or plant. How are you alike? How are you different?

Friends

Agree or disagree: Parents should have a say in their son's or daughter's choice of friends.

Things, Things, Things

Agree or disagree: Young people today are too materialistic.

Superstitions

What superstitions do you have — or what superstitions do people you know have? Why do you think those superstitions exist? How do they affect you or others?

Sadness

Describe a time you felt sad, unhappy or depressed. What happened? How did you act? How did those around you act?

Excitement

Describe a time you felt excited. What happened? What made you excited?

Laws

Agree or disagree: Laws are a waste of time.

Happiness

Describe a time you felt really happy. What happened to make you happy? How did you act? What did you do? What did others involved do?

Disappointment

Describe a time you felt disappointed. What were you expecting? What happened instead? How did you react? What did you do?

Music

My kind of music is . . .

Loneliness

Describe a time you felt lonely or left out. What happened? Why did you feel lonely or left out? What did you do?

Injustice

Describe a time you felt unjustly or unfairly treated. What happened? Why was it unfair? What did you say? What did you do? What did others do?

Commercials

What TV commercials do you enjoy? Why? Which ones do you hate? Explain.

Best Book

One of the best books I've ever read is . . .

Frustrated

Describe a time you felt frustrated. What frustrated you? What did you do about it?

Computers

The best thing about computers is . . .

The Down Side

The worst thing about computers is . . .

Courage

To me, what really takes courage is . . .

Hamburgers or Broccoli?

Agree or disagree: Being a vegetarian is a good idea.

A Perfect Pet

Describe the perfect pet. What animal would it be? How would it behave? What would you name it? Where would it sleep?

More Materials from Cottonwood Press . . .

Did You Really Fall into a Vat of Anchovies? — and Other Activities for English and Language Arts, edited by Cheri Armstrong, is a collection of games, seasonal materials, projects and activities that are far from run-of-the-mill. For example, students will love creating personal brochures about themselves or writing modern versions of the legendary witches' brew from *Macbeth*. Other activities include "Video Journals," "Frosty Sheds Old Image," "The Melting Teapot," "Playing Around with Country Music" and more. Grades 5-9 (and up).
Order #VATB4 ....$18.95

Ideas that Really Work! — Activities for English and Language Arts, by Cheryl Miller Thurston, is a potpourri of materials that will make your life easier. It is very adaptable and includes activities at different levels of difficulty, grades 6-12. The wide variety of activities are interesting and unusual. Some titles include: "Cars in Class," "Word Snapshot Posters," "Mythological Monsters," "Grammar Ideas for Teachers Who Hate Teaching Grammar" and much more. Best of all, the ideas really *do* work with students. Give them a try!
Order #IDB4 ....$21.95

Hot Fudge Monday — Tasty Ways to Teach Parts of Speech to Students Who Have a Hard Time Swallowing Anything to Do with Grammar, by Randy Larson, is filled with quirky humor, clear writing and unusual approaches to studying parts of speech. The activities allow students to be creative, to have fun with language and to learn about parts of speech *as they write*. Don't be surprised if your students understand the material in **Hot Fudge Monday** better than anything else on the market about grammar. Grades 5-9 (and up).
Order #HOTB4 ....$18.95

Row, Row, Row Your Class — Using Music as a Springboard for Writing, Exploration and Learning is a collection of activities that combines English and language arts with the power of music. It includes a wide variety of activities, most involving writing. "Was Clementine Really so Darling?" has them telling the whole story of ballads and folk songs. With "Rapping Rapunzel" students rewrite fairy tales as rap songs. Other activities include "Singing the Blues," "Jukebox for the 1990s," "Public Service Rap" and much more. Grades 5-12.
Order #RRB4 ....$12.95

The Case of the Colorful Kidnapping — a Read-aloud Play about Brothers, Sisters and Bullies, by Cheryl Miller Thurston, is a funny and revealing play, both about dealing with siblings (including stepbrothers and stepsisters) and about dealing with "tough guys" who may not be as tough as they seem. The play runs about 25 minutes and includes parts for 15 characters. Best of all, it includes eight activities for further writing and discussion, all centered around problems faced by today's students in a changing and often-difficult world. For grades 5-8.
Order #CKB4 ....$12.95

Writing Your Life — Autobiographical Writing Activities for Young People, by Mary Borg, is a gold mine of materials that help students enjoy writing. The book encourages students to explore their lives and their thoughts, helping them learn about who they are and who they would like to be. Students enjoy activities like "Before You Were Born," "Who Are You — Really?" "Brag Page," "Family Tree," and "Life's Highs and Lows." We have been amazed at the flexibility of the open-ended activities in this book. Grades 6-12.
Order #WYLB4 ....$14.95

Journal Jumpstarts — Quick Topics and Tips for Journal Writing, by Patricia Woodward, contains the most practical material you are likely to find on the subject of journal-writing in the classroom. There are more than 200 topics to help "jumpstart" your students when they need help finding something to write about. The author has suggestions for grading, handling confidential material, keeping up with the reading, dealing with complaints, giving credit and much more. For grades 7-12.
Order #JJB4 ....$5.95

Short and Sweet — Quick Creative Writing Activities that Encourage Imagination, Humor and Enthusiasm about Writing, by Randy Larson, is a book of 28 reproducible creative writing activities. The activities help students of all ability levels have fun with writing as they stretch their imaginations. Most activities can be completed in less than a class period, with time left over for sharing — an important part of the creative writing process. Some titles: "Endangered Pumpkins," "1-900-PIMPLES," "Tabloid Times" and much more. Grades 5-9 (and up).
Order #SSB4 ....$10.95

Surviving Last Period on Fridays and Other Desperate Situations, by Cheryl Miller Thurston, is full of language arts games and activities that are interesting, challenging and educational — never busy work. **Formerly published as the *Cottonwood Game Book*,** this useful resource has just been revised and updated. All the games and activities are ready to photocopy and use tomorrow. A few titles: "Pass Back Stories," "Crazy Sentences," "Holiday Challenge," "Space Race," and much more. Grades 6-9 (and up).
Order #GB4 ....$14.95

When They Think They Have Nothing to Write About, by Cheryl Miller Thurston, is an invaluable source of writing ideas. **Formerly published as the *Cottonwood Composition Book*,** the book has been completely revised, updated and expanded. Some of the titles: "Sick! Sick! Sick!," "What to Do with a Glopsnerch," "The Rock Concert" and much more. There are 25 ready-to-photocopy assignments, complete with prewriting activities, and 101 quick writing topics suitable for short assignments or journals. Grades 6-9 (and up).
Order #CB4 ....$14.95

Games for English and Language Arts, by Cheryl Miller Thurston, is a collection of reproducible games. The games include everything from oral and group games to word puzzles and creative challenges. Just a few titles: "Cars," "Alphabet Trade Names," "Ik," "Rhyme Time," and "Bill Cosby Meets the Slimy Rubber Band Monster in the Center of Mom's Microwave" and much more. Help your students discover the pleasure of playing with words, language and communication. Grades 6-9 (and up).
Order #GELB4 ....$16.95

My Personal Yearbook is a perfect project for homeroom — or for your regular classroom. Students will love completing their own copies of this fully-illustrated and inviting book. Unlike most Cottonwood Press books, **My Personal Yearbook** is not reproducible. That's because it is designed for each student to create his or her own unique, personal book of memories. The 52-page book makes a popular special project for students at any time during the school year. Low-priced, particularly when purchased in quantity. Grades 5-8.
Order #YB4.....................$6.95 for one copy. (Call for discount prices.)

Order from Cottonwood Press TODAY!

Quantity	Item #	Name of Item	Price Each	Total Price

Shipping & Handling

Add		Add	
$10.00 & under.................................. $1.00		$45.01-$75.00.................................$5.50	
$10.01-$25.00.................................$2.25		$75.01-$100.00...............................$6.50	
$25.01- $35.00................................ $3.50		$100.01-$250.00.............................$8.00	
$35.01-$45.00.................................$4.50		$250.01-$350.00.............................$12.00	

Merchandise Total	
Colorado residents add 3% sales tax	
Shipping &Handling (see chart)	
TOTAL	

Call us!

1-800-864-4297

By calling our Toll-Free Hot Line, you can . . .

- quickly order with Visa, MasterCard or a school purchase order.

- request a free catalog — mailed immediately to your home or school.

- learn about our current specials.

- talk to knowledgeable and friendly sales representatives.

Name _____

School _____

Address _____

City _____ State ____ Zip Code _____

Method of Payment:

___ Payment enclosed ___ Visa ___ MasterCard ___ Purchase Order

Credit Card # _____

Expiration Date _____

Make checks payable to:
Cottonwood Press, Inc.
305 West Magnolia, Suite 398
Fort Collins, Colorado 80521
1-800-864-4297

If you enjoy our products,
tell your friends about Cottonwood Press.